My Book of

Metaverse

Investing

A Complete Beginner's Guide to

Understanding the Metaverse and How to

Invest (Stocks, Virtual Land & NFTs)

Gerald Hinkle

Disclaimer

The information in this guide is for educational purposes. And should not be misconstrued as personal financial advice.

The author shall not be liable for losses incurred as a result of the application of the information in this guide.

All data provided were correct at the time of the writing of this guide.

Always trust your financial advisor for personalized financial advice.

All trademarks are properties of their respective owners. And the author of this guide has no affiliation with any of them.

CONTENTS

INTRODUCTION

What is the Metaverse? Every day, we keep hearing new words in this ever-evolving technology space. Some months back, we were battling with NFTs and their meaning. Today, it seems we have moved a notch higher and are now talking of the Metaverse.

But what is this Metaverse that everyone is talking about? Is it yet another buzzword or fad that will fade soon? Well, let's see.

In my usual manner, I have used this short guide to explain what the Metaverse is. I do this all the time for new technologies. My guide on NFTs has helped hundreds of people around the world grasp the concept of that great crypto innovation.

You can check out the NFT guide here. And the good thing that distinguishes me from the other writers in this space is that I use the simplest language that anyone can understand to drive my points. I also make use of relatable everyday scenarios to explain otherwise complex issues.

That said, what is Metaverse?

In recent years, there has been an increase in interest in permanent shared virtual worlds. Facebook's creator, Mark Zuckerberg, has said that creating a metaverse is a realization of a concept he had and was interested in before he began working on social networking.

Microsoft, on the other hand, has declared that it is developing a corporate metaverse. But what exactly does it imply? That's precisely what we'll be looking at in this guide.

We'll look at what Metaverses are and how you may profit from them. When I expose individuals to new topics, I do this all the time. I don't only explain an idea to them; I also teach them how to gain from it.

So, let's get this party started.

CHAPTER ONE

What

Metaverses as a concept have been around for a while. They're like a digital shared world where we may adopt whatever identity we like or collaborate on projects together.

Metaverses haven't always been portrayed as beneficial. The phrase was originally used in Neil Stevenson's Cyberpunk film Snow

Crash, where it was used to describe a location where people go to escape the drab authoritarian reality of their everyday lives.

It's where robots put us once we've become their slaves so they can use us to create power in the Matrix movies. These are probably not the first concepts that spring to mind when it comes to Silicon Valley's own views of the future.

However, it's evident that we've been working towards this notion since the advent of the internet, social media, virtual reality, and early efforts to create shared digital landscapes like Second Life.

Zuckerberg has defined the Metaverse as an internet that you are inside of rather than merely looking at, which gives us some insight into how he plans to approach it.

We're having serious discussions about Metaverses right now because a number of significant technological trends have matured to the point where they'll be up to the challenge.

Virtual Reality is undoubtedly one of them. Since purchasing Oculus in 2014, Facebook has made significant investments in virtual reality. The company has not made it a secret that it does not believe VR's future will be limited to the walled gardens of gaming and education, where it is now most prevalent.

Instead, according to Zuckerberg, the ultimate objective is to combine virtual reality's capacity to construct virtual worlds with the power of social media to create shared online places. This has been done previously - for example; there are several VR applications that enable you to socialize with your pals.

The distinction with a metaverse is that users aren't always constrained to the app's intended activity, such as conversing or playing a game together.

Instead, gamers should be allowed to do anything they want in virtual reality. The objective is to develop virtual worlds that mimic as much of our surroundings and reality as possible, similar to the world depicted in Ready Player One, a science fiction adventure film.

The Metaverse should accommodate emergent user behavior rather than being confined or developed for a single purpose, such as virtual reality tennis simulations or collaborative working platforms like Slack or Teams.

Metaverses don't have to be confined to a single platform as long as there is a shared, uninterrupted experience. Your metaverse existence might take you from intense VR worlds to 3D scenes reproduced on a standard flat screen to 2D apps on your cell phone, depending on what you choose to do.

In terms of the user experience and other target control, an essential element of the Metaverse is that there is consistency across activities and surroundings.

Everyone appears to agree that avatars will play an important role in the metaverse. You must have some type of digital avatar for others to engage with in order to match Zuckerberg's idea of being in the metaverse ecosystem. Your profile image serves as your avatar on Facebook and other social networking networks.

It may be a 3D depiction of you in the Metaverse. It might be anything you can imagine in a game or fantasy metaverse, but one crucial idea is that this avatar or some aspect of it will be able to travel across and between various sections of the Metaverse. And, no matter what you're doing or what platform you're on, this avatar will be identifiable as yourself.

This isn't only about technological advancements anymore; there is all indication that the Metaverse is becoming a reality already. Since the outbreak of the pandemic, many individuals have become more reliant on the internet to conduct their lives. We've become used to working, buying, and socializing online.

As a result, putting all of these activities together in a single seamless digital environment isn't as far-fetched as it would have been a few years ago. However, these developments also pose social concerns.

From identity theft & fraud to trolling & abuse, the transition to online life has definitely permitted a lot of activities that may be harmful or unhealthy.

There's also the possibility that real-world disparities, such as the income gap, may be duplicated in the Metaverse.

Immersive 3D worlds need a lot of computational power to create; thus, people with a limited budget for headsets and computer equipment may have a less enjoyable experience. If, for example, firms make employment choices based on a person's existence in the Metaverse, this might severely influence society. Or if it becomes a platform for delivering education or even dating chances.

When?

When is it going to be a reality?

So, how far away from the Metaverse are we? The firms who are genuinely considering establishing Metaverses are all framing it as a future goal.

For the time being, it mostly serves as a conceptual model for how current online environments like social media or work-based environments like Nvidia's Omniverse might become more immersive and thoroughly interwoven into everyone's life.

The initial stage will almost certainly be to combine virtual reality with social networking. Facebook has lately made a lot of noise about its plans to achieve this, claiming that it expects to be able to do so within the next five years.

However, it's evident that there are still a slew of issues to be resolved before we're ready to transfer our whole lives online.

While many activities such as shopping, entertainment, socializing, and working are being carried out in digital settings, we are not yet at the technical or societal level where we are ready to do the same with the bits that connect them all together.

For the time being, there are ways to get a taste of what a metaverse experience would be like. Epic Games has experimented with extending the Fortnite game realm to encompass social events and concerts, the most recent of which included Ariana Grande.

Some people just see the Metaverse as the internet's next generation. What will the internet be like when 2D displays are replaced by headsets or even lenses that transmit pictures straight into our retinas?

The fact is that everything is still up in the air. When networked immersive worlds become our online home, no one knows what the architecture or regulations will be.

However, with the largest names in tech vying to give us their vision, we should anticipate more interest in the notion.

Summary of the Chapter

The Metaverse is best defined as the next major internet iteration, similar to how the mobile internet was created on top of the regular internet in the 1990s and early 2000s.

It's essentially an unlimited network of linked virtual worlds where people can work, interact, and play using VR, augmented reality, and other technologies.

There are a few key aspects of the Metaverse worth mentioning.

1. There will be no time restrictions or lengths: the Metaverse will never be turned off; it will never be unavailable due to server maintenance or restarts.

People will be able to login and exit at any time without having to load or preserve their data. Everyone will be able to experience and live in the Metaverse at the same time.

The closest example I have for you is that in 2019, Fortnite staged an in-game concert where you could go witness DJ Marshmello perform a virtual set for the duration of the game if you checked in at the time.

That sensation may have been shared by everyone who was playing at the time. If you're on a voice chat with your pals at the moment, it'll seem like you're all at a Marshmello performance at the same time.

The Metaverse aspires to be like that, where everything happens in a single moment, and millions of individuals may interact with each other in a digital/physical reality.

2. The Metaverse will have an economy: With so many people spending time in this digital AR and VR reality, both companies and individuals will be able to offer products and services.

Consider a famous company selling digital items in the Metaverse. Louis Vuitton, for example, may be selling a digital bag that your digital avatar may use.

Within the Metaverse, I'm confident people will be able to start their own modest enterprises. A user-run casino, for example, is a common business model in practically every sort of online multiplayer game.

As a result, attention is monetized in this fashion, and the more attention that enters the Metaverse, the more chances for transactions will arise.

3. Endless possibilities for user-created content: although companies and businesses will undoubtedly generate experiences and material in the Metaverse, individual users will significantly impact the bulk of the Metaverse's content.

Thanks to a user-created content paradigm, the Metaverse may also be very scalable and constantly current to the newest trends.

Besides user-created content, many firms, like Nike and Microsoft, have already hopped on board the rising excitement around the Metaverse.

Nike filed seven trademarks with the United States Patent and Trademark Office in late October 2021 for downloadable virtual products, retail shop services containing virtual goods, non-downloadable virtual footwear, and so on.

Within the Metaverse, we can already witness some institutional acceptance of digital commodities, which leads me to my next argument.

4. Everything will be interoperable, spanning both the digital and physical worlds: augmented reality and virtual reality will be essential components of the Metaverse. The first thing that springs to mind is Amazon's augmented reality view.

Customers may visually preview things in their homes before making a purchase using Amazon's AR view. This notion isn't entirely unfamiliar to us at the moment, but it may exist in the Metaverse.

Another intriguing use is that items will be able to be traded in the Metaverse with other commodities that use the same platform, independent of community or branding.

Consider a scenario in which you could swap a precious Fortnight skin for something that would go in your digital house, like a digital sofa. Essentially, all borders will be broken down, and this is what the Metaverse is all about.

Let's speak about how to invest in the Metaverse now that you know what it's all about.

CHAPTER TWO

Investing

We learned about metaverses in the previous section.

In this part, I'll show you the various ways to profit from this growing sector.

Early adopters are generally the ones who earn the most money in every new sector. Reading this book, you may position yourself to be an early adopter of the metaverse business.

You must learn how to profit since just understanding how technology works should not be sufficient.

When I discuss an invention, I usually do it this way. I'll show you what it is and how you may benefit from it. I did the same in my NFT guidebook. You can find the book here.

That said, there are a variety of ways to invest in the Metaverse and generate money, and we'll go through each one.

Before we begin, let me state unequivocally that this is not financial advice. I am not a certified financial planner. The NFT, crypto, and investing worlds are all very dangerous.

As a result, please do your own study and make your own choices.

Now, there are a variety of ways we might begin investing in the Metaverse at this early stage. These are some of the methods that will be used:

- Purchasing cryptocurrency tokens that support the Metaverse
- Purchasing in-game NFTs
- Purchasing land/properties within the Metaverse
- Stocks – publicly traded stocks of companies that support metaverse infrastructure

These are all ways to profit from the metaverse. So let's get started with the very first point.

Cryptocurrency tokens

Various crypto coins currently support the metaverse.

If you go to CoinMarketCap or CoinGecko and choose "Metaverse," you'll find a list of the current metaverse tokens available on the platform. You'll see a screen similar to the one shown below.

Take a look at the first four tokens in the screenshot above. Market capitalization is used to rank the coins. Axie infinite, Decentraland, Sandbox, and other projects are plainly visible.

In a way, all of them are creating their own metaverse. Decentraland and Sandbox are constructing a true metaverse, but Axie Infinity will also deliver LAN gaming, potentially serving as a metaverse.

These tokens are used to make in-game purchases of assets. Let's imagine a customer wishes to purchase a certain NFT; they'll need to use a token like Illuvium to do so.

Many individuals are buying these tokens in the hopes that these platforms will one day become the most popular metaverses. This is similar to a stock in certain ways.

I realize it's not the same as a stock, and you don't own anything in the game you've invested in. You don't own Decentraland or Sandbox, but you are basically holding a stock-like asset that supports the real development of these games. In the picture above, we can see several of these unique tokens.

We noticed a tremendous gain in value from the original pricing of some of these tokens once Facebook announced that they would be renamed to Meta.

Let's take a look at $MANA, for example. The value of this token was roughly 79 cents. The token jumped to a new all-time high of roughly $3.50 (at the time of writing) after Facebook's rebranding to Meta, which is absolutely absurd. In the play-to-earn (P2E) gaming sector, we noticed a number of these tokens behave in the same way.

The same thing occurred with Sandbox, another Metaverse that is now under construction. Following Facebook's statement, the value of the token skyrocketed.

By acquiring the token that supports in-game purchases and the ecology of these metaverses, you will effectively be gaining some exposure to these games.

In-game land

Purchasing in-game assets is the next method to invest in the metaverse. We're going to speak about land, particularly here. No, I'm not referring to actual land.

In some of these metaverses, you may buy land parcels. You may be able to start a company using these lands. You may create games, parties, your own house where your avatar can relax after a long day of partying in the metaverse, and much more.

Sandbox and Decentraland are two excellent examples of platforms that enable you to accomplish this (purchase land).

The Sandbox home page is seen in the screenshot. A button titled "Map" may be found on the left side of the page. If you click on the map, you'll be led to a virtual environment where you may buy land pieces or plots in this game.

The wonderful part about this is that you can use a profile photo to show who purchased the property.

When you look at the map, you'll see that some people have bought land. You may also view the land that has not yet been sold. When you acquire such plots, you may utilize the area to construct Sandbox events, activities, or games.

Decentraland also has its own version of this. They have their own map that we can look at, as well as their own marketplace, where we can buy Decentraland chunks or plots of land.

Take a look at the image below.

OpenSea.io is currently one of the sites where you may buy some of the Sandbox lands. Then there's Decentraland, where you can acquire assets via their own marketplace. They both have highly busy discord servers where you can talk to other people and perhaps purchase or sell land.

One of the coolest aspects of in-game real estate is that you own it. You own the property in the game just as you own the property you're presently living on in real life. And inside these games, you have complete control over the property and land you possess.

With these plots of land, we have the capacity to create a wide range of experiences.

Furthermore, since these plots of land are restricted in number, there will only be a specific quantity of land available in these games.

So, even if Decentraland and Sandbox develop into large games with vast player numbers, there will always be a finite quantity of land available in these games. As the number of individuals playing these games grows, so will the demand for these lands and people wishing to buy their own plots of property.

As I previously said, one of the ways to get exposure to metaverse investment is to purchase one of these plots of land, which may rise in value in the future if demand for these plots of land develops.

NFTs

Purchasing NFTs is another option to profit from the metaverse. However, we'll be discussing wearables and in-game assets other than land in this section.

If you're unfamiliar with NFTs, check out this guide that explains everything about it here.

Now, avatars in a metaverse will have some apparel - genuine things and accessories that they will use to represent themselves in that environment. Specific assets might be NFTs that are only available in those metaverses.

Let's have a look at a couple of markets to get a sense of what I'm talking about. Let's take a closer look at wearables.

For example, when you visit Decentraland,

you'll discover that they have a specialized collectibles store that includes wearables and avatars used on the network. Some of the apparel items are also limited edition.

Still on Decentraland, if we go to the marketplace and check in the artifact area, we'll find Artifact Studios, a well-known Decentraland creator who makes wearables.

The majority of the wearables are one-of-a-kind pieces. According to some of the collections, only roughly 10,000 of these assets will ever exist as an NFT inside Decentraland. So, like land, they're limited-edition products with the potential to become popular inside a metaverse.

As the user base for these sorts of games expands, or as the popularity of artifact firms' assets rises, more people will want to buy them, raising their value.

In real life, people want to express themselves via clothes, accessories, and other stuff that they wear on their bodies. It won't be any different in a metaverse, which is an online reality. So, in a sense, digital wearables will be a method for us to express ourselves and flex.

So, instead of wearing a Rolex watch in real life to impress people that care about that kind of thing, we can wear a bored ape yacht club sweatshirt or an artifact studio shoe to communicate that degree of flex inside these metaverses.

I'm bringing this up because, depending on the demand for these assets, their value might grow. As a result, purchasing some of these assets will almost certainly earn you money as demand for them rises.

You can also profit from speculating on Axies on the Axie infinite marketplace.

The Axie infinite marketplace is shown in the picture below, and you can see some of the in-game materials on the marketplace.

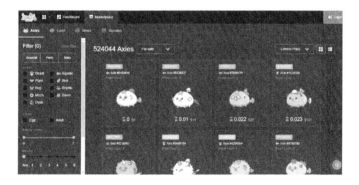

NFTs may be utilized in Infinity games, and some of these individual assets are NFTs. Depending on their rarity, some of these Axies may sell for thousands, if not hundreds of thousands of dollars.

The key reason these Axies have value in the first place isn't only because some of them are collectible. To play an Axie infinite game, you'll need an Axie. As a result, these NFTs enable game participants to efficiently play a certain game.

There are also in-game assets that will be utilized for Lunacia's LAN gaming whenever it is released. And these in-game assets will be NFTs as well. They might potentially increase in value based on the asset's utility inside the game and the amount of demand it generates.

We may see a rise in the value of some of these NFTs if the user bases for these games continue to expand and the popularity and demand for particular products that bring value or some sort of prestige.

Now, let's talk about the next way to get started investing in the Metaverse: buying stocks that support the infrastructure and development of these metaverses.

Stocks

Although the Metaverse is still a few years away, there will be firms and stocks that are critical to its development. And in this part, we'll look at those businesses.

There's a good probability that some of these firms may see rapid expansion as a result of increased demand for their products or services.

As a general recommendation (this should not be construed as personal financial advice). That said, let's get started.

Matterport

This is a world-class spatial firm that digitizes the real world. Their present company uses cameras to capture real estate, digitize the data, and create 3D models of the properties.

Realtors may then utilize these models to present to customers without ever having to set foot in a property.

The necessity to digitize and integrate every physical feature of the actual world into a virtual environment will be one of the Metaverse's toughest problems. That's where Matterport enters the picture. Within 10 years, it might be one of the most powerful actors in the metaverse.

It now controls the rapidly expanding industry for the 3D digital transformation of the real world into the digital world. So, until a rival just does it better, I don't see Matterport being obsolete very soon.

Matterport currently owns 38 patents and 28 pending patents, making it very difficult for new rivals to join the market. SAS, or subscription as a service, presently accounts for 52 percent of Matterport's income. Matterport's broad client base is also a good feature; with less than 10% of total income coming from the top customers and 330,000 customers across all sectors, the company's revenue is not strongly influenced by any one customer.

Redfin, Century 21, Airbnb, Hyatt, Autodesk, and a long list of other firms have partnered with Matterport.

Matterport does certainly have a collaboration with Facebook A.K.A. Meta, according to their last earnings calls on November 3rd, 2021. To build AI systems for the physical and digital worlds, Matterport has teamed up with Meta AI research.

Surprisingly, when looking at Matterport's price, the tale seems a little questionable. Matterport is already a highly valued firm, with a 52 price to sales ratio and a market worth of 4.9 billion dollars.

When compared to its trailing 12-month sales of 105 million dollars, the 4.9 billion dollar market value is a lot of valuation for a small amount of money. According to one of their investor calls, the adjustable market is expected to be around 240 billion dollars, and they estimate they've only penetrated approximately 4% or slightly less than 4% of it.

Matterport's EPS and sales were somewhat below expectations on their earnings call, as I indicated before.

They started trading down roughly 6% after hours as a consequence of those results. So, despite the poor results, if you are optimistic about Matterport in the long run, this might be a good time to purchase.

Unity

Unity is the next stock you might check into. This firm provides software that allows developers to build and commercialize games across 20 platforms, including Windows, Android, iOS, PlayStation, and others.

The Unity platform is presently used to develop around 60% of AR and VR games. While gaming generates the bulk of Unity's income, the company is attempting to diversify its revenue streams.

Unity bought Metaverse Technologies, a 3D optimization software business, in the second quarter of 2021. Professional creators will be able to load 3D data into Unity more simply and rapidly, allowing them to optimize models for real-time development.

Unity is currently experiencing some value and profitability issues. The firm makes a lot of money, and it grows year after year. Their gross margins are still strong, but R&D spending has dragged down their net and operating margins. They're investing heavily in themselves, which is definitely a positive thing, but their metrics may seem to be lacking in the near run.

Unity has a liquidity buffer of roughly 1.6 billion dollars that they may utilize to cover losses in the interim, even if they won't generate a profit for a long time.

The stock now represents strong growth expectations with a price to sales ratio of 39, an enterprise value to sales ratio of 44, and a price to book ratio of 21.3.

When compared to other firms in its industry, it is now trading at a premium.

Over the last three years, Unity's revenue has grown at a compounded annual growth rate of roughly 142 percent, but experts estimate it will increase at a pace closer to 29.3 percent over the next 10 years. With such rates of growth, the present value may be justified. The average analyst price objective currently ranges from 116 to 130 dollars per share.

The bottom line for Unity is that the stock is not cheap, but it has a strong revenue growth rate and a massive army of monthly active users across all sorts of Unity apps, totaling roughly 2.7 billion. That's a lot of users, and their sustained success in other areas might really justify the increased price tag.

As a result, both Unity and Matterport should significantly influence the Metaverse.

Facebook and others

Apart from the two firms mentioned above, Facebook is another company worth keeping an eye on.

Facebook is now constructing its concept of what a metaverse should include, and they have opted to become a metaverse firm.

In addition to Facebook, other tech businesses to watch out for include Apple, Nvidia, and Roblox. All of these firms are presently working on metaverse infrastructure. There will be a slew of others as well.

It will be your responsibility to do research and determine whether other publicly listed corporations are entering the metaverse market and seeking to support it.

Metaverse Index

We discussed metaverse tokens earlier; in this part, I'll show you a fascinating technique to potentially gain exposure to many of these tokens that support the Metaverse. We can do so via a platform called the Metaverse Index. Take a look at the screenshot below to see how the platform appears.

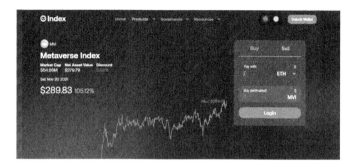

This platform functions similarly to an index for publicly listed equities, except it is for play-to-earn gaming metaverse tokens.

The platform compiles all of the main metaverse tokens into a single ERC20 token index.

The image below shows the many coins that the index holds in its portfolio.

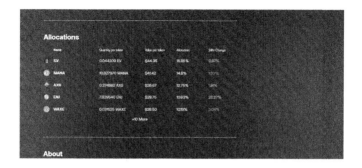

If you simply want to gain exposure to metaverse-related coins in general, you may end up buying into the metaverse index instead of buying each and every one of the tokens seen in the picture and introducing further risk to your portfolio.

With some of these tokens, you won't witness the explosive 10x, 20x, 3x, 5x, or whatever x growth you may expect. The argument is simple: purchasing from an index dilutes the tokens, making them a safer and more consistent gamble.

They are, however, the kind of things I like investing in since I am a less risky person than many others.

I'm sure some individuals reading this book won't want to become engaged with high-risk assets in the crypto industry or in general. Buying from an index like this one might be a good way to get started buying and investing in the metaverse without taking on too much risk.

WRAP UP

You've just seen a few options for getting started with metaverse investment. The metaverse has a lot of people thrilled right now. Since Facebook made that statement, it has undoubtedly become a catchphrase, and many people can see themselves being engrossed in this online world.

Furthermore, many individuals are eager to take advantage of the chance to be this early and invest in the metaverse or metaverse-related assets. But it's also worth noting that this is still all quite risky.

We have no idea which of these metaverses will be successful. Furthermore, NFTs and cryptocurrency, in general, are a risky asset class. Just because I mentioned these topics in this tutorial doesn't imply you should spend your whole life savings in the metaverse.

It's still quite risky, so do your homework and make your own conclusions. It'll be fascinating to watch how this all plays out, and I'm personally quite thrilled since I believe this is the internet's future.

If you have found this guide useful, then you would definitely want to get my NFT guide.

It is titled: How to make money with

NFTs: Everything You Need To Know About Making Money with Non-Fungible Tokens Without Creating Your Own Crypto Art

It has helped a lot of other people like you grasp the concept of NFTs. And I am sure it will do the same for you.

Many readers all over the world commend my writing style for being direct and straightforward. I use everyday language to explain otherwise complex stuff and make it understandable for anyone, irrespective of their knowledge level. And if you enjoyed reading this guide, you will enjoy reading my other guides too.

Lastly, do not forget to leave a review on this book's Amazon page. It will help other readers like you decide on getting this guide.